SECTIONED

Poppy Radcliffe

Dear Peter
Enjoy & thanks for
watching me live
Poppy

ABOUT THE AUTHOR

Despite having been sectioned six times in five years, Poppy Radcliffe is most definitely not insane. She's a perfectly ordinary girl with an extraordinary past. A past peppered with turmoil, heartbreak, psychosis and an insatiable appetite for life. In this collection her focus is mainly on the subject of mental health and her anger at a system that she feels fails so many brilliant people as they either settle down into acceptance of their prescribed limitations, become so medicated that they cannot function without care, or are left to rot for years with no end in sight.

This collection focuses on the human psyche, especially the workings of the brain at times of peak stress. Most of these poems have been written in or shortly after release from mental wards. She is proud of them; when read back they conjure up true feelings and when recited they have been well received, so she is excited and honoured to share them with you.

In the coming years Poppy will be working on a book of a similar name incorporating these poems into the narrative that inspired them.

For her future poetry she is aiming to focus on topics of gender, sexuality and relationships as she commences on her own journey of discovery at the tender age of forty. These most likely won't be out until post 2025. In the meantime, why not check her out on social media and try and catch her at an open mic night?

Instagram: @poppyradcliffe

Tik Tok: @poppy_radcliffe

YouTube: Illusions of Grandeur

Blog: sectioned.me.uk

DEDICATIONS

To Rosalind Burns

Your tutelage at school and constant support since has given me the strength to keep a belief in myself at times when others doubted me.

My spelling still hasn't got any better, thanks for doing the proofread.

To Hollis Dixon

Your writings were an inspiration to me at a time when I felt I had nothing, they spoke to me. I hope you see similar worth in my own. Thanks for convincing me to never give up.

To the rest of my friends and family

You have been anything from horrendous to angelic and I love each and every one of you. Thank-you for being on this journey with me.

Special mention to Judy Humphrey, Dave Nash, Asher Cummings and Hanbury Hampden-Turner for going above and beyond the call of duty.

With thanks to

Cover Photograph: Flash Bang Wallop

Cover Design: ZigZag Creative   Works

CONTENTS

WILL YOU HEAR ME THEN?

Do you want a suicide note?
I've got one 300 pages long.

No. I don't want to die.

I want to cruise the Caribbean,
Have lovers around the world.
I want to write, sing, dance and push my career to its limits.

But if you stop me
If you say I can't have the life I had
If you say I can't kick back and relax
If you say I can't laugh at myself, at you, at life
I will stab myself in the head
Carve "Slut" into my arm
And slit my throat in front of you.

And don't ever say I didn't tell you why
I've been telling you for years.

All you had to do was listen
And if you can't listen; read.

They won't let you be normal and that makes people insane

MISSION STATEMENT

I didn't want to weave a web
I didn't want to save the world
I didn't want to scream and shout
Or turn my body inside out

I wanted just the quiet life
To have a job and be a wife
To maybe have a kid or two
And spend my life alone with you

But life is strange and sticks and stones
Despite them words will break your bones
But words can change a life around
And put your feet back on the ground

And words with nothing left to lose
You have a life, you live, you choose
And now I choose my soul to bare
At least I try, at least I care.

INNOCENCE DESTROYED

I sit here and I hate myself
I don't want meds, I don't want help
It used to be a better day
Until they sectioned that away

Until they stripped me of my soul
Spent weeks and months and years
Convincing me that I was wrong
That I was ill, somehow undone

"I drank too much", "I screwed too much"
Somehow my brain just didn't work
Funny that, it seems to me
It always had been fine

I'd got my grades, I'd done my job
I always had performed
And crucially upon it all
I <u>liked</u> my deranged mind

And now there's anger in my soul
A pain I can't abide
A hardness and a broken heart
An innocence destroyed.

THE AFTERMATH

Of course, I know that I'm insane
It ever was the way
But never did I mean to find
So much anger, nor such pain

But love hurts
Plane flies
Lullabies
Your love destroyed my soul

And now I need my medicine
Because in the world of untold lies
Truth hurts
Judgement dies

Deranged and random
Messed up thoughts
Three a.m. waffling
Trying, trying - oh the loss.

NICE

You're nice
It's an understated word
Not exciting or bold
But nice

You're kind
Not thrills and spills
But kind

You're gentle
And that's all anyone can ask

Just gentle, kind and nice
And with that comes peace
And with peace
The universe opens a path

You're nice
I like nice.

IF I COULD LIVE AGAIN

If I could live this life again
I wouldn't change a single thing
I'd maybe dream I had more balls
Or fought more battles, climbed more walls

I'd maybe have a tat or two
Or dreads or funky tartan shoes
I'd maybe pierce my nose or lip
Or ride an awesome acid trip

Or leave the real world behind
And find myself in Kazakhstan.
If that was then and this is now
The who, the what, the when, the how

I wouldn't be the girl I am
The girl who thinks she is a man
The girl who through the darkest day
Has family and friends who stay

The girl who wallows through the night
And in the day picks up the fight
The girl whose love is pure and true
Who knows that she would die for you.

LET ME FLY

I do not want to smoke
I don't want to drink
You're not helping me fly
You're making me sink

I want to impress you
To teach you to dance
But rather than listen
You're making me prance

It's not God my lovelies
It is just the wind
But sometimes it happens
The wind gives you wings

I love you all dearly
Don't want life alone
But I'll live like a nomad
Till I find my home.

PRETEND

I'll pretend to be happy
I'll pretend to be glad
I'll pretend to be anything
Anything but sad.

I'M GETTING THERE

I'm sitting here
The room's a mess
The remnants of my great distress.
Please don't clean it for me now
I'm getting there
I'm getting there.

FOR LOUISE

Beneath a mask of smiles
An ocean full of pain
She wants to live a happy life
They think that she's insane

The world's full of beauty
The human realm's a mess
She hides wearing baggy jumpers
She'd rather don a dress

Let her face the music
Come on, give her a chance
Don't keep her wrapped in cotton wool
Stand back and let her dance.

AN IMPATIENT SOUL'S LOST SHADOW

In a wondrous world Julie screamed
The essence had run dry
Where once was joy and butterflies
Now seemed like dust and dirt and lies

With chaffed bare hands and battered knees
She scratched the arid earth
Digging deeply frantically
A shallow puddle to unturf

For Julie felt that if she found
Some water underground
She could renew the arid earth
So life and beauty would abound

Yet nothing came but lice and stones
And clouds of swirling black
Her tears the only liquid here
The bright Sun burning on her back

The memories of sweet release
Of frolics, fun and friends
Of dabbled dew and lily pads
Of woodlands, fields, dunes and fens

These urged her onwards, deeper down
So desperately she dug
Not heeding any pleas to wait
She travelled further through the mud

The small oasis Julie found
Was far below the ground
Quite shut off from the world above
A shallow joy of broken love

And then the rains began to fall
Water flowed down the walls
But nothing good this deep could grow
An impatient soul's lost shadow

The raindrops splashed her face and neck
And laughed at her distress
She screamed and clawed and tried to climb
But was far too deep down the mine

The arid earth began to bloom
Larks, daisies, sweet perfume
Lush grass and verdant meadows too
Pools, and tadpoles, a life anew

And as the world above rebound
Julie was nowhere to be found
A pitiful and hollow sound:
Alas. In the well, Julie drowned.

IF NIGHT WERE DAY

In a forest far away
A little girl began to blow
She blew so hard she moved the trees
And brought them crashing to their knees.
She did not mean to, but she did
And what was done was not undid
She blew so hard she puffed with fright
And ran off screaming to the night

In the darkness she could not see
The scary quest of destiny
She hid among the shadow beasts
And gorged with plenty at their feasts
Her heart was clear, her head divine
But something tingled in her spine

She knew this way she could not stay
And sometime soon she'd face the day
The sun would rise and cast anew
A carnage that she knew she blew
She ran and hid and closed her eyes
But nature saw beneath the lies

Nature saw deep within her soul
All ripped and torn - a gaping hole
A hole that could not fill itself
A hole too large for just one elf
She stumbled and she dared to move
One foot then two she faced the blue

She saw the pain around her go
And started some new seeds to sow
What once was waste began to bloom
But days were short and night too soon
If only night could become day
The world could live another way

Then out of darkness sprang the light
A communal zone of such delight
A sanctuary to call her own
With others who had blown and blown
And flowers came and friends appeared
And one by one they calmed her fears

The faceless few became a mass
And darkness ran and hid and gasped
The sun shone down upon her face
All tainted red with her disgrace
But not alone she had new strength
A world that now would not be drenched.

WARRIOR

I'm like a warrior poised for battle
Sitting
Waiting
Sitting
Thinking
Knowing that I might die
Weary from the war already fought
Thinking that this may be the time
I don't come back
Sitting
Waiting
Sitting
Thinking
Ready
Planning
It's been so long
It's been so hard
The battles fought
The battles lost
A glimmer of hope.
Here we go
Over the top
One last push
Fight
Onwards

Stand.

TEMPTATION

Who, who, who, who is he?
The one I close my eyes and see?
The one who's always there but never comes
Who beats the sound of knocking drums

Raggy doll why do I let you in?
You're a serpent, the snake I want within
The snake that slithers up my thighs
Promises me paradise

The serpent fills my loins with lust
Resist, resist his silky touch
And push him back towards the dust

But I can feel and it's left a stain
A nest of darkness planted deep
Ready to burst and through my body seep
The snakes invade and turn my hair to blazing flame

They'd win if I was on my own
Temptations inside every bone
I'd cave, I'd crawl, I'm scream, I'd moan
I'd find you under every stone

But I am stronger than you think
And time will soothe with every blink
Not alone, I will survive
The thoughts inside will soon subside.

DUMPED

I dared to dream, (to live again)
That I'd found someone to ease the pain
I dared to hope I wasn't alone
That someone nice might throw me a bone

Someone might help me day to day
Someone might once show me the way
They'd help me from my knees to feet
And show me how I could defeat
The demons that control my mind
The pain that shivers down my spine
The fear that causes my eyes to weep
My feet to drag
My back to steep

I know, that it's a lot to ask
But is it really? Time will pass
And so I'll walk this land alone
And slowly, slowly, turn to stone.

THE DRINKER

Don't say I'm not a drinker
For that I really am
The outward face of sobriety
Well, that one is the sham

For when I am on my own
It's all I think about
The luscious golden liqueur
That takes away my doubt

That allows me to forget
That leads to fitful rest
That takes the days asunder
And clears them off my chest

Don't say I'm not a drinker
For I drink every day
I don't know how to carry on
I cannot stay this way

Don't say I'm not a drinker
But take my hand and laugh
And tell me that we'll change this
That I'm on the right path

For sure I will defeat this
I'll do my very best
But now I'd like some vodka
And fitful awful rest.

CRACK DEN

So, I wander to the crack den
'Cos that's where my pain ends
I'd thought it'd be a happy day
I thought I'd make amends

I booked a nice hotel suite
Thought I would treat myself
But there's no one here to share it
I'll stay here by myself

So, I'll wander to the crack den
Maybe then I'll ease my pain
That all the friends I still cherish
Don't feel for me the same

I'd walk many a country mile
I'd knock right on their door
If that was what was called for
I'd even do way more

But I invite them round for dinner
Or just a cup of tea
And yet everyone's too busy
Too busy to see me.

So, I'll wander to the crack den
And drink the cheap red wine
And drown away my sorrows
Until they think I'm fine

It may take many moons
It may take many years
To alleviate the terror
To soothe the constant fears.

I have smartened up my terrace
The place is looking tight
But no one there to visit me
Well, isn't that just nice?

So, I'll wander to the crack den
'Cos that's where my pain ends
I thought it'd be a happy day
I thought I'd make amends.

PRAY

I act like the predator
But I am the prey
Don't ask me why
God made me that way.

BETRAYAL

If you could see my scars
You'd know I'd been betrayed
If you could see my scars
You'd know that I'd been flayed

You'd hide your kids away
You'd tell them, "Babe don't look"
She's so very damaged
Some kind of hidden crook

If you could see my scars
You'd turn yourself away
Hiding your repulse
Unsure of what to say

But you can't see my scars
So let us play pretend
Everything is always
Alright in the end.

BETRAYAL 2

Please stop asking questions
My mind simply can't take it
You don't know better
You haven't read
The books I gave
The links I sent

Don't tell me that you love me
Don't question my insight
For love based on fear
Is no love at all.

LIBERTY

It's not fair when you blame me
For the hurt in your life
It's not fair when you blame me
For your troubles and strife

It's not right when you tell me
That I must be polite
Then start screaming in my face
And disregard my fright

It's not fair that I'm in here
I always worked so hard
It's not fair that I'm locked up
While you play all the cards

It's not fair that my insight
Is now classed as despair
It's not fair that all my pain
Makes you rip out your hair

For it's you who have hurt me
Some mistakes are okay
But promise me you will not take
My liberty away

I love you, yet I hate you
There's so much more to say
But in here I must die, you
Took my liberty away.

HELP

Don't tell me that you're helping
When all your help is nothing thus
When your help is only punishment
And nothing based on trust

Don't tell me that you're helping
When you can't do the simplest thing
If you will not get me my laptop
Maybe some nice long string?

Don't tell me that you're helping
When you're just watching your own back
While mine is all red, raw and bleeding
And my heart set to crack

Don't tell me you don't see them
The hopeless, disenchanted mass
The ones that now no longer struggle
Just lie upon the grass

Don't tell me you can't see it
The constant pain behind their eyes
Which sparkles with a gleam like raindrops
When someone stops, says "Hi".

So do not make me say it
For you will not accept my words
Just let me lick my wounds in peace
And make it through at least

So...........

Don't tell me that you're helping
When all your help is nothing thus
When your help is only punishment
No place to lay my trust.

DEATH

Oh, why am I still here Lord?
I died so long ago
Why make me walk this world now?
Trapped in death's sorrow

The endless onward grind Lord
When I've already peaked
The time that you took my soul
Then put me back on feet

I walk this world in silence
A pain I can't repress
Wishing that death would take me
Let my fake smile rest.

I didn't die!

PROLOGUE

You ask me for my fantasies
I say the quiet life
With a clean house and gardening
With baking instead of strife

I've been there now. I have done it
I've done near everything
So let me tell you of the things
That would cause my heart to sing:

I want to bake a pretty cake
Maybe a rainbow one
With coloured icing and sprinkles
And a bow that I have done

I'd like to plant some daffodils
In bright delightful pots
And maybe a thriving herb patch
I would like that, lots and lots

I dream of chores not being chores
The hoover, dust, and mop
And maybe even ironing
The housework that God forgot

And as the evening hours lengthen
I'll scribble, draw and write
Give the little cat a cuddle
And make a tasty bite

I'd like to bake a fancy flan
A hotpot for the main
When I tell of you my fantasies
They're really most mundane

Of course, I like the passion
A party's mostly fun
But I would like the wholesome life
Now all that's done is done.

Thank-you and good night!

Printed in Great Britain
by Amazon